Every vehicle
on the

i-SPY

D0865980

INTRODUCTION

Motor vehicles are everywhere and, as there are about 35 million vehicles registered for use on British roads – of which almost 30 million are cars – it means there is roughly one vehicle for every two people.

You'll easily recognise the difference between a car, a van and a truck or lorry, but have you ever looked at them really carefully? With the help of this i-SPY book, you'll begin to notice just how many different 'species' of car, commercial vehicle, tractor and motorcycle there are in everyday use … as well as plenty of other unique vehicles that are like nothing else you'll find. Some of them are built for certain jobs – others are just for the fun and enjoyment of driving or riding.

We have arranged these 120 vehicles, most of which you'll find in Britain and many other countries, in alphabetical order by the names they're most commonly called. Before you start to collect your i-SPY points for spotting them, have a good look through the book and get to know the differences. There will be no mistaking a police motorbike or a milk float, of course, but many of the vans and trucks have the same shape at the front, around their cabs and passenger compartments. The differences start just behind the doors. Tractor units (cabs) detach from their load and look very different when not pulling trailers. Look out for them as you travel around.

Keep a special eye out, too, for the many trailers in the book. Most of them are commonly found in Britain, but you never know what sort of vehicle might be towing them; it could be a great chance to double up on your i-SPY points!

Make sure you look carefully at all the cars you see, too. There are saloons, estates and hatchbacks everywhere, but it's not every day you'll spot a limousine, a supercar or an electric city car.

How to use your i-SPY book

We've included pictures of most of the kinds of vehicles you're likely to come across on the roads in Britain. They're arranged in alphabetical order. You need 1000 points to send off for your i-SPY certificate (see page 64) but that is not too difficult because there are masses of points in every book. Each entry has a star or circle and points value beside it. The stars represent harder to spot entries. As you make each i-SPY, write your score in the circle or star.

ADVERTISING VEHICLE

Jordan Tan / shutterstock.com

Many vans and trucks have advertising on their sides, but look out for unusual adverts. It could be a car with a gigantic drinks can on the back or a van painted like a cow, complete with horns on the roof, door mirrors shaped like ears and eyebrows over the headlights!

AMBULANCE

Points: 15

Ambulances are covered in a bright, eye-catching and reflective livery that, along with the blue flashing lights, warns other drivers to let them pass by on their way to an emergency or when urgently transporting a patient to hospital.

Points: 10

ARTICULATED LORRY

This is one of the largest vehicles found regularly on the road. A front tractor cab unit pulls a trailer with two, four or six wheels; this trailer can be flat with a visible load, or with its cargo enclosed.

BENDY BUS

Points: 20

These articulated buses can be seen in London and at many airports. They pivot in the middle and are known as bendy buses. More passengers can be accommodated inside them than in standard single-decker buses.

4

Points: 5

BICYCLE

The typical bike has a triangulated frame which gives it the strength to support the rider, and wheels with lots of spokes that spread the impact from the road through the tyres. A mountain bike like this one has knobbly tyres so it can be ridden over rough ground.

BLOOD/ORGAN DELIVERY BIKE

Top Spot! Points: 40

Because it's manoeuvrable and unlikely to be held up in traffic jams, a powerful motorbike is the best way to get urgent materials to a hospital. This could be blood or even a body organ, such as a heart, that might save someone's life.

BOAT TRAILER

Points: 20

Many kinds of trailers are available to transport boats on. They vary with the size and weight of the craft, from simple frames for a small dinghy to large, multi-wheel models that can transport a powerboat or even a small yacht.

Points: 10

BUS, DOUBLE-DECKER

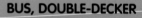

Buses with an upstairs compartment operate in every part of Britain. They're big, rectangular and able to carry lots of people. Some have two sets of doors, front ones for entrance and rear ones for exit to help passengers flow on and off.

BUS, SINGLE-DECKER

DavidGraham86 / Shutterstock.com

You'll see single-deck buses everywhere, smaller ones sometimes have one set of doors for passengers, while larger ones may have two. Increasing numbers are low-floor vehicles, which are more accessible for wheelchairs and pushchairs.

CAMPER VAN

This compact mobile home is adapted from an ordinary minibus. You'll be able to tell a camper from a minibus by looking at the roof: camper vans generally have an extendable roof that extends upwards so you can stand up inside the van when parked. Even when folded flat, you can still see it.

CAR REMOVAL TRUCK

Points: 25

This lorry has a platform at the back called a flatbed, and its own crane that is used to lift cars on to the flatbed. You might see one removing a crashed car … or an illegally parked car in a city centre!

Points: 15

CAR TRAILER

One way to transport two cars with just one driver is to use a car trailer. These trailers are made from strong-welded metal so they can support the weight of the car.

CAR TRANSPORTER

These incredible articulated lorries can carry several cars – usually brand new ones being delivered to garages – on up to three levels. The cars are driven on to the back of the transporter and then locked into place; they look like they might fall off but are safely secured!

CARAVAN

Points: 15

Owning a caravan means you can go on holiday and take your home with you, giving you freedom to stop anywhere you choose. The range of models is enormous, from tiny two-wheelers to four-wheeled mobile mansions!

Points: 30

CARAVAN, FOLDING

A folding caravan has an upper section that retracts to reduce its height almost by half. The interior fittings cleverly interlock so nothing gets crushed. It fits inside a garage and its low profile means a car uses less fuel when towing it.

CAR-DERIVED VAN

Points: 10

A very practical option, particularly for small businesses. The body shell is the same as a normal car, but the rear side windows are replaced with metal panels, and instead of a rear seat there is a flat load area.

CATTLE TRAILER

Points: 25

You see these large trailers in the country, where farmers use them to move cattle as well as sheep or pigs. Slots in the sides allow plenty of air so the animals can breathe well, while twin axles give good stability on fields or rough tracks.

Points: 20

CONCRETE MIXER

Art Konovalov / shutterstock.com

If you see one of these large vehicles rumbling along the road, it's probably on its way to a building site. The huge drum at the back revolves as the truck drives along, keeping its mixture of·sand, cement and water moving so it can be poured out at its destination as concrete.

This type of vehicle could be handy in orchards – its rising platform allows access to ripe fruit in treetops – hence the name. But they are used for all kinds of 'working at height' tasks, including repairs to streetlights and telegraph poles, and maintaining buildings. Some have extendable 'feet' that lift the vehicle off the ground, making it totally stable when the platform is raised.

Points: 15

CITY CAR

These short, stubby cars are ideal for people who live in large towns and cities because they can make use of short gaps in traffic, tight parking spaces and usually have economic engines.

CLASSIC CAR

Points: 20

Classic cars are those built from 1945 to around 1980 and have a loyal band of enthusiastic owners dedicated to keeping them going. Classics are often identifiable from their chrome trim and their often rounded styling.

Points: 5

COACH

There is never any standing room on a coach because it's not designed for constant stop/start operation. Coaches are used on longer journeys. Seats are arranged in pairs either side of an aisle.

CONTAINER LORRY

These lorries, with flat rear trailers, are the last link in the global container shipping chain; cranes transfer the containers from cargo ships to the lorries, carrying all types of goods all over the world.

CONVERTIBLE

This type of car has a roof in the form of a folding metal frame, covered with flexible canvas-type material. Some are electrically powered like this Mini, others need to be raised or lowered by hand. Some convertibles now have folding metal roofs.

Teddy Leung / shutterstock.com

COUPÉ

This Audi TT is a typical example of a coupé. It has a roofline that tapers to a finish at the very back of the car. Most coupés have a roof lower than a family car. But many still also have two small seats in the back.

CROSSOVER

A 'crossover' has a lower half that's like a 4x4 off-roader and an upper portion like a normal family hatchback or estate. Many come with four-wheel drive. Popular models include the Mazda CX-7, Ford Kuga, Nissan Qashqai and Peugeot 3008.

Yauhen_D / shutterstock.com

A pretty common sight on UK roads if you know what you are looking for, this kind of lorry is perfect for regular, small deliveries of heavy items. That's why they are popular with breweries transporting barrels of beer to a large number of pubs. The side curtains can be pulled aside easily so goods can be unloaded from either side without the need to empty the whole trailer.

DOG HANDLER'S VAN

Dog handlers' vehicles look like any other van on the outside, apart from one key feature: a revolving roof-top ventilator, ensuring the animals travelling inside get enough fresh air and keep cool.

DRAWBAR TRAILER

Weight and length restrictions mean there are legal limits on the size of articulated trucks on our roads. For bulky but light cargo, however, a drawbar trailer – towed behind a truck with a rigid chassis – can increase carrying capacity.

DRIVING SCHOOL CAR

People learning to drive must display a square, white sticker with a red 'L' on the front and back of the car, telling other road users that they are 'Learning'. Driving school cars are easy to spot as they usually have large adverts or roof signs that also draw attention.

DROPSIDE PICK-UP

Art Konovalov / shutterstock.com

Builders find these small trucks useful. At the rear is a flat load area on to which pallets of bricks, for example, can be loaded by a forklift truck. The side and rear panels then fold up and lock into place, to prevent anything sliding off when the truck is moving.

ELECTRIC CITY CAR

This Reva G-Wiz is a tiny 100% electric-powered car, which classifies as a 'zero-emission vehicle'. This means the owner is exempt from the London Congestion Charge, and can enjoy benefits like free parking and battery recharging.

EMERGENCY RESCUE VEHICLE

If a car breaks down while on a journey, the driver can contact an emergency rescue organisation who will send out a mechanic in a van. The mechanic will try and fix the car at the roadside, but if that isn't possible the car will be secured on to a trailer and towed to a nearby garage.

Points: 5

ESTATE CAR

This type of car is designed for dual-use. With the rear seats in the upright position, it's like any other family car, but when they are folded it can carry very large loads.

Art Konovalov / shutterstock.com

EXCAVATOR

Points: 20

Its proper name is a 'back-hoe loader', which describes its two functions of being able to dig at one end and shovel at the other. But most people call it simply a JCB after the name of the company that makes most of them.

EXECUTIVE CAR

People who have important positions in companies and other organisations often drive cars that look impressive, with large wheels and a prominent radiator grille. Popular brands include Audi, BMW, Jaguar, Lexus and Mercedes-Benz.

FASTRAC

Top Spot! Points: 40

JCB make this powerful, four-wheel drive tractor that can also be used as a road vehicle, which is why it has full-width plastic mudguards fitted. It can be driven at 40mph on tarmac, much faster than conventional tractors, and can do all kinds of jobs, from ploughing to towing. You may see these on country roads travelling between farms.

FIRE CONTROL UNIT

Britain's larger fire stations have a fleet of different vehicles for each type of incident. This VW Transporter is operated by the London Fire Brigade, as a fire investigation unit. It carries special equipment and staff trained to assess a situation before, during and after the fire itself.

Points: 20

FIRE ENGINE, PUMP

Everyone calls them 'fire engines' but the main task of a vehicle like this is to act as a powerful pump. It carries its own water supply for putting out small fires and can also pump water from the mains supply. Lockers along the sides carry protective clothing and specialised rescue equipment, and ladders are carried on top.

FIRE ENGINE, TURNTABLE

Points: 30

This impressive vehicle is found in larger fire stations, especially in cities where there are many tall buildings. Although it carries firefighting equipment, its main job is to offer an escape route from upper storeys of buildings. The boom on the back can be raised upwards, so people can step to safety on to the platform on the end of it.

Points: 10

FUEL TANKER

Bulk liquids are transported in specially designed vehicles called tankers. They come in many sizes but some of the biggest are used to deliver fuels from refineries and depots to petrol stations. The tank itself is rounded, and shaped so that every last drop can be drained out of it. There are also tankers that are used to carry powder.

GLASS VAN

Points: 20

It doesn't take much to shatter a sheet of glass, so transporting it can be difficult. Window companies use a van like this, with a specially designed frame attached to its side that gently grips even very large glass panes so they arrive in one piece.

Points: 15

GRITTER

On the back of this truck is a triangulated container, wide at the top and narrow at the bottom. It is filled with fine chunks of grit and, when moving, the driver spreads it on the road surface. A gritter is essential when roads are covered in snow or ice to keep vehicles moving.

GT CAR

Art Konovalov / shutterstock.com

This car is a Maserati GranTurismo. It is built in Italy and is very fast. GranTurismo is the Italian for Grand Touring. GT sports cars can cover, or 'tour', long distances at high speed.

Points: 5

HATCHBACK

A hatchback has an additional door across the rear end, opening on to a luggage space that can be doubled in volume if the rear seats are folded down. Their practicality has made them one of the most popular types of car on the road.

A hearse is a specially lengthened type of large estate car used to carry a coffin. They often travel slowly and in convoy with other vehicles, containing relatives and friends. Most hearses are black but other colours such as silver and gold are becoming more common. They are usually made by luxury brands. This one is a Mercedes-Benz.

Points: 10

HEAVY LORRY

These lorries, called Heavy Goods Vehicles or HGVs, can have more than two axles; some have steering to the front two to help them get round tight corners. Drivers need a special licence to drive one.

HIGHWAY/MOTORWAY MAINTENANCE TRUCK

Points: 20

This general-purpose truck helps to prepare major roads and motorways for disruptions and roadworks. It carries cones and barriers, and thanks to its powerful lighting rig at the back can act as a gigantic warning signal.

Points: 20

HORSEBOX

At first glance it might look like a removal van, but it has a ribbed ramp for a rear door that folds down so horses can be led easily inside. Many horseboxes also have a cosy compartment above the cab where riders can sleep at events a long way from home.

ICE-CREAM VAN

Points: 10

The brightly painted vans have a tall rear end section where you can buy your ice cream through a sliding window. Score double points for one with a large model of an ice cream cone on the roof.

Points: 25

KIT CAR

Very few people can afford an original classic sports-racing car from the 1950s or 1960s. But you can build a replica in your own garage. This Westfield Eleven kit car is a reproduction of a 1950s Lotus.

LIGHT MILITARY VEHICLE, LAND ROVER

Points: 15

The original four-wheel drive, go-anywhere utility vehicle, a Land Rover is so versatile that it can be used on battle fields as well as farm fields. Score double for one in army camouflage paint.

LIGHT MILITARY VEHICLE, PINZGAUER

EW 94 AB

These are built with four or six wheels, all of which are driven so that the Pinzgauer, with its vast ground clearance, can negotiate almost any terrain. For this reason, they are popular with the British Army, which owns several hundred.

LIGHT TRUCK

This Iveco Eurocargo, along with the DAF LF, is among the UK's most popular light trucks. They deliver all sorts of the things we need locally every day, such as fresh bread and groceries.

Points: 30

LIMOUSINE

This is an extra long saloon car with very wide doors and a luxurious interior. They are often driven by a chauffeur. Some limousines have an extra row of seats and an extra pair of doors. 'Stretch limos' have an extended chassis and are an increasingly common sight.

Teddy Leung / shutterstock.com

LONG-DISTANCE COACH

For long journeys, perhaps from one country to another, special coaches are available. They tend to be very large vehicles with two decks of seats and on-board facilities including toilets and a kitchen to make the trip pleasant. Three axles make the ride more comfortable and allow a heavier payload. The lower rear section is used to carry luggage.

Points: 20

LOW-LOADER

Very powerful 'tractor' units are needed to haul a low-loader trailer like this. It's a basic platform-on-wheels used for transporting heavy machinery or vehicles from place to place.

LUTON VAN

A Luton van has a load area extending out above the passenger compartment. This type of van was created in Luton, Bedfordshire in the early 20th century. The town was Britain's hat-making centre, and the local manufacturers needed a van for carefully carrying headgear that was light but bulky.

Points: 20

MICROCAR

These miniature cars come mostly from France. Smart, Aixam, and Ligier are all brands that are sold in the UK. They're also known as 'quadricycles'. Their tiny engines mean they are slow, but fuel consumption is low and they are ideal in towns.

MICROVAN

You will see many of these tiny delivery vans in use even though they're no longer sold new. The driver and passenger sit above the low-power engine, which puts the cab in the 'forward control' position. They're ideal for small businesses making daily deliveries in tight city streets.

Points: 30

MILITARY TRUCK

The military operates these four-wheel drive trucks, which can haul either a load of equipment in the back or provide covered seating for 18 soldiers.

Here is a great opportunity for your i-SPY points total… but only if you have good hearing and are prepared to get up early! These near-silent electric vehicles deliver milk and other products in urban areas in the very early morning. During the daytime, they are recharged to be ready for their next delivery rounds.

Points: 10

MINIBUS

Some schools have their own minibuses, and others are used by Scout groups, sailing clubs and similar organisations. A typical minibus, like this one, is converted from a delivery van, with windows and seats added. You can hire one if you need it only occasionally.

MOBILE BANK

Top Spot! **Points: 40**

Internet banking is perfect for those who live in remote parts of the UK, but a mobile bank is a great alternative for people without online access. Inside is a proper counter, situated just behind the driver's compartment.

Points: 25

MOBILE CRANE

You'll see these amazing vehicles driving from one construction site to another. They fold up, rather like a Transformer, but when needed the crane can raise and extend telescopically for all kinds of heavy lifting tasks.

MOBILE LIBRARY

Points: 25

Not everyone lives near a library, so many local councils offer a mobile book-borrowing service – they bring the library to you, especially if you live in the countryside. These special truck-based vans are fully kitted out with bookshelves and all the latest titles.

Points: 15

MOBILE SNACK BAR

Motorways have service areas, other major roads have cafes and restaurants, but you'll find mobile snack bars in lots of other places. They generally have a serving hatch at the side, with a fold-out canopy and counter, through which your bacon sandwich, fish and chips, cup of tea or can of fizzy drink is served.

MOPED

Points: 10

Old style mopeds were a low powered motorcycle with pedals. You won't see many of those today – they're no longer sold. Instead, a modern moped will be like this Yamaha Aerox R, a mini-scooter for commuting that, despite its modest 49cc engine, can still be customised to look cool.

Points: 10

MOTORCYCLE

This is a Honda Varadero, which only has a 125cc engine but has excellent handling and styling like a bigger sports bike. A streamlined fairing ahead of the handlebars helps shield the rider from the wind and the rack above the rear wheel can be used to strap on a small item of luggage.

MOTORCYCLE, TOURING

Points: 15 15

Some motorbikes are designed for zipping around on but others, like this Triumph Rocket III Classic, are big-engined touring bikes. Large and comfortable, but also powerful, there is plenty of room for two people – the passenger is called a 'pillion' rider.

MOTORCYCLE COMBINATION

Points: 35   Top Spot!

Minxav / shutterstock.com

A motorbike with a sidecar is known as a combination. The sidecar is a single-wheeled vehicle that is attached to a motorbike and used to carry a passenger. They have been produced in Britain for over a hundred years and are still being made today.

MOTORHOME

Points: 10

10

Many holidaymakers find it easier to drive a motorhome than a car pulling a caravan. They are equipped with kitchens and some have toilets and showers. This one has a sleeping compartment above the driver's seat.

10 **Points: 10**

MULTI-PASSENGER VEHICLE

These 'MPVs' are packed with features making them ideal for large, busy families. The biggest models have three rows of seats so seven or even nine people can be carried. Many have sliding rear passenger doors and removable back seats. MPV can also stand for multi-purpose vehicle.

PAVEMENT/ROAD CLEANER

Points: 15

15

You'll see this tiny truck in towns and cities, where it is used to suck up rubbish from gutters and pavements. The brushes at the front sweep up and a suction machine underneath pulls it into a collection box at the back. Some machines can also hose down dusty streets with water.

Points: 10

PICK-UP

At the front, it looks like a normal saloon car, but the bodywork is abruptly ended behind the doors and a large open-topped tray is fitted – the pick-up bed. They're widely used for small businesses and in the countryside.

PICK-UP DOUBLE-CAB

Points: 15

15

This utility vehicle is a useful mixture of car and pick-up truck. There are five proper seats inside the four-door passenger compartment but the shortened pick-up load bay is still spacious enough to carry plenty of stuff.

Britain's forces use similar cars to everyone else, although with heavy-duty suspension and special communications equipment. You can't see that technology but you can see the reflective 'Police' livery all over the bodywork (usually a white or silver base colour), and the blue flashing warning light unit on the roof. They use a variety of models depending on the job, from hatchbacks and estate cars to four-wheel drive Sports Utility Vehicles.

POLICE MOTORBIKE

Points: 15

This 'bike is a BMW 1200 RT, a large, powerful yet nimble sports model that has a proven track record with police riders across Britain. Apart from the eye-catching luminous yellow livery, a police bike is recognisable by its substantial radio antenna on the back, pannier storage units on both sides above the rear wheel, and the flashing blue lights on its fairing; plus, of course, the policeman or woman riding it!

Points: 10

POSTAL VAN

Like the pillar-box you drop your letters into, the vans used by Britain's national postal service, Royal Mail, are all painted red. Some have a yellow stripe along the side but they all carry the Queen's crown-shaped crest. This is one of Royal Mail's smaller local delivery/collection vans; it also uses bigger vans, minibuses, light trucks and articulated lorries.

PRISONER TRANSPORT VAN

Points: 25

For carrying people between police stations, courts and prisons, a special van like this is used. It is, in effect, a mobile prison cell designed to ensure that criminals can't make their escape. They travel with guards in the back in a secure metal 'cube', built on to the back of a reinforced van cab. Police motorcycles are often used as outriders to clear the way for this type of vehicle.

 Points: 25

QUAD BIKE

It looks like a four-wheeled motorbike, and that's exactly what a quad bike is. Although it has the stability of a car, it is steered by handlebars and the rider sits astride a saddle and sometimes wears a helmet. They are very useful for farmers and shepherds, the fat tyres and four-wheel drive allowing them to go anywhere.

RADIO CAR

Broadcasters need specially equipped cars for covering events and on-the-spot news reporting. The enormous antenna on the roof allows journalists to transmit their reports back to the studio. There's usually a webcam mounted on the roof, and plenty of room inside to carry equipment, and also to conduct interviews.

Points: 20

RECOVERY TRUCK, FOR CARS

This is a light commercial vehicle, based on a van or light truck, with a flat bed at the back on to which a broken-down car can be winched. A strong nylon rope is attached to the front of the car, and it's then pulled aboard up a pair of extendable ramps that pull or fold out from the back of the truck. It can then be taken to a garage for repairs.

RECOVERY TRUCK, FOR TRUCKS AND BUSES

Points: 25

A broken-down truck or bus can cause huge disruption for other drivers. That's when one of these large, strong vehicles is needed. The rear end has a drop-down rig that can be positioned under the front wheels of the stricken bus or truck, and it can then be carefully towed away. It has powerful warning lights on top.

Points: 25

RECYCLING COLLECTION VAN

This van-based vehicle has separate compartments at the back so different categories of rubbish can be carried back to the council depot, to make sorting it out easier. You may see larger vehicles that take away unsorted waste for recycling, but most will carry a recycling slogan along their sides. Score for any 'recycling' vehicle you see.

REFRIGERATED/FREEZER VAN

Points: 20

This van has a special 'cool box' on the back designed to carry food that must be kept in freezing or chilled temperatures. You can tell it apart from a normal van because it will have a visible refrigeration unit protruding from the roof or front of the chilled area.

Points: 15

REFUSE TRUCK

These large, noisy trucks visit your street usually once a week or once a fortnight. The wheelie bins are lifted automatically and their contents tipped into the back where an automatically operated mechanism compacts it so as much as possible can be crammed in.

REMOVAL VAN

Points: 20

If you've moved house then a huge truck like this probably took care of the job. Removers have special ways to position all your possessions so nothing gets damaged on the journey. Some have a sleeping compartment above the cab.

Points: 35 **Top Spot!**

RICKSHAW/BIKE TAXI

mikecphoto / shutterstock.com

Three- and four-wheeled rickshaws are a tourist attraction as taxis around central London. The passengers sit at the back under a canopy while the 'driver' is at the front, steering with handlebars and providing all the power – through pedals! They are the ultimate in zero-emission transport.

ROAD-SWEEPER

Points: 15

The tank at the back is filled with water; the driver sprays this on to the road and uses the brushes at the sides to collect the rubbish, at the same time damping down dust and cleaning the road. As they move slowly, there is normally a flashing orange light on top.

Points: 5

SALOON CAR, FOUR-DOOR

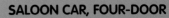

For many years, this was the traditional shape of car. Known as a 'three-box' car: one in the middle for the passengers, a smaller one sticking out of the front for the engine, and a third for the boot. These days boots tend to be less boxy!

SALOON CAR, TWO-DOOR

A two-door saloon with the same three-box profile will still have at least four seats, the rear ones accessed by tipping the front seats forward. This style of car, typified by the BMW M3 shown here, tends to be aimed less at families and more at drivers who like sporty performance. That's why many two-door saloons are marketed as coupés.

Max Earey / shutterstock.com

Points: 15

SCAFFOLDING TRUCK

To carry the long steel poles of scaffolding, special flat trucks or trailers are required. Around the edges of the flatbed load area are uprights that stop the poles rolling off when they're being transported. These trucks also carry the metal joints that allow vertical and horizontal poles to be joined securely together, when renovating buildings.

nhrssergne / shutterstock.com

SCHOOL BUS

Local councils organise special bus services to take children to school – maybe you use one. This bus operates in London. School buses in the USA are all painted yellow; in the UK, the way to spot one is to look for the yellow 'School' sign in the window or the words 'School Service' on the destination board.

SCOOTER

These compact motorcycles are very popular for commuting, as they can beat traffic jams and use minimal fuel. This one is made by Yamaha. It's typical of the modern scooter in that it has sleek styling but is simple to use.

SECURITY VAN

It seems like a basic delivery van but look closely and you'll see it's been toughened up with armour-plated doors and thick bullet-proof glass. It also has side-mounted video cameras and hefty protective strips and wheel arches. It's all to make the van more secure as it collects and delivers money and other valuables.

Boloncici / shutterstock.com

Points: 15

SKIP TRUCK

Skips are huge, metal buckets that can be delivered and collected by trucks like this six-wheeled DAF 55, which has a special hydraulic lifting mechanism at the back to lift the skip on and off. The weight it can lift is awesome!

SNOWPLOUGH

Top Spot! **Points: 40**

You'll only see a snowplough after a major snowfall, so spotting them is pretty tricky. The big blade at the front is specially curved to lift snow off the road and push it aside. These trucks often have a gritter unit on the back.

Points: 15

SPORTS CAR

A sports car has two seats and a folding fabric (although sometimes metal) roof. This makes it great fun for journeys on fine days. Sports cars, like this Mazda MX-5, are built close to the ground, and the low centre of gravity helps it corner at high speed.

SPORT-UTILITY VEHICLE

Points: 10

Most people call them simply SUVs. An excellent combination of road car suspension and chassis, with high ground clearance, big wheels and often four-wheel drive technology, means they are great off road and on.

Supercars are high powered sports cars that have blistering acceleration and can often have a top speed of over 200mph. There are many different manufacturers of supercars including Aston Martin, Lamborghini and De Tomaso. Some are famous International Motor Sport manufacturers that specialize in supercars only, like Ferrari and Mclaren, but other more familiar car brands like Audi and BMW also have their own supercar models. The car shown here is the Ferrari 458, a mid-engined supercar that can go from 0–60mph in three seconds and has a top speed of around 210mph. You might see a supercar being driven on a race track as well as on the road.

SUPERMARKET DELIVERY VAN

Points: 10

Most large supermarket chains have a home-delivery service for internet. They use refrigerated vans to deliver their goods. You can easily spot them by the adverts on the van sides.

Points: 10

SUPERMINI

The term 'supermini' arose in the early 1970s, when car designers tried to improve the original, fun-to-drive Mini but with more space and practicality. These hatchbacks are still very popular today.

TANDEM

Points: 30

gabriel12 / shutterstock.com

This is the name for a bicycle built for two people. They are great for cycling holidays, and some enthusiasts even race them. The person on the front has to trust the person behind is pulling their weight; likewise, the person on the back relies on their friend up front to steer and brake!

TAXI

Britain is one of the few countries that builds a special taxi, rather than a converted car. An 8m (25ft) turning circle means it can tackle narrow city streets, where many of them operate. Notice the roof sign: when it's not lit, the taxi is in use; when it's illuminated it's available for hire. If you need a taxi, you have to wave to the driver.

THREE-WHEELED CAR, FRONT SINGLE WHEEL

Points: 30

This Reliant Robin was the UK's most popular three-wheeler. It's very light, with fibreglass bodywork, which means, legally, it's classed as a tricycle and can be driven on a motorbike licence. Last on sale in 2002, owners still like it because it's economical and rustproof.

THREE-WHEELED CAR, BACK SINGLE WHEEL

EVG 867-Y

Much less common than a Reliant-type three-wheeler is a car with its single wheel behind the driving seat. This British-made Triking might look odd but it's similar to three-wheeled sports cars of the 1920s and '30s. It has a powerful motorbike engine sticking out of the front and, with a little practice, is great fun to drive.

Points: 50   Top Spot!

These small delivery vans are brilliant for light deliveries in busy cities. Previously they were much more popular in Europe and in the Far East but they are now catching on in the UK too.

TIPPER

Points: 20

This eight-wheeled truck is one of the biggest tipper trucks you'll see on the road. Its big, open container at the back can tip out its massive load of loose material such as sand, gravel or stones using a heavyweight hydraulic ram behind the cab. At the back, a hinged tailgate swings open to regulate the flow.

TRACTOR

Points: 10

Most tractors feature huge rear wheels with knobbly tyres and a glass-sided cab from where the driver has an all-round view. This is essential because it may be called upon to tow trailers, plough fields or dig trenches.

Points: 20

TRACTOR CAB

Not to be confused with an agricultural tractor, these units are the powerhouses that pull containers and flatbeds around the country. They can look quite strange when they are travelling without pulling a load.

TRAILER, FOR DOMESTIC USE

Points: 10

A trailer can be attached to the back of any car that has a tow hook, and plugs into the car's electric system to power its lights. It's very handy for carrying holiday luggage or camping gear.

A tram is half bus, half train. Like a bus, it travels along city streets, but like a train its wheels run in tracks and it usually draws its power from overhead electricity cables. Most trams are articulated with two or three sections allowing them to carry many people in busy town centres without the need for extra buses.

UNIMOG

Top Spot!   Points: 50

The Unimog has been manufactured for many years in Germany by Mercedes-Benz. It is a tall four-wheel drive truck that combines pick-up and tractor abilities. The base unit can be fitted with many kinds of bodies, and power take-off (PTO) points mean it can perform unusual tasks, such as roadside hedge-cutting.

Points: 5

VAN

Route66 / Shutterstock.com

You will see vans like this Ford Transit, the most popular of its type in the UK, absolutely everywhere. They are simple workhorses with an integrated cab and load area, and come with two, side-opening back doors or, sometimes, a lifting tailgate. Other models are LDVs, Peugeots, Renaults, Vauxhalls and Volkswagens.

VETERAN CAR

Owners treasure these ancient cars from the veteran period, which ran from 1885 to around 1905. Every year, the London–Brighton Veteran Car Run on the first Sunday in November is the place to see lots of them. They may look very basic, but these were extremely modern cars back in 1900!

VINTAGE CAR

Top Spot!   Points: 40

Vintage cars were made from 1918 until 1930, at a time when few British people could afford a car. They are very valuable among collectors. You're most likely to see one at a car show in the summer.

WALK-THROUGH DELIVERY VAN

Points: 20

This is a large van used by laundry companies and courier services. Its height is necessary so the delivery driver, who will make many calls over a working day, can easily walk into the rear compartment from the driving seat, to pick up a package carried in a racking system.

Points: 30

WIDE LOAD ARTICULATED LORRY

This vehicle is a monster lowloader for carrying things that are extra-wide, such as a mobile home as shown here. It is very low to the ground and has several wheels on which to spread the weight. If you see something like this driving slowly along a motorway it sometimes has a police escort in order to prevent other traffic getting too close.

INDEX

i-SPY

How to get your
i-SPY certificate
and badge

Let us know when you've become
a super-spotter with 1000 points
and we'll send you a special
certificate and badge!

HERE'S
WHAT
TO DO!

(✓) Ask an adult to check your score.

(✓) Visit www.collins.co.uk/i-SPY to
apply for your certificate. If you
are under the age of 13 you will need
a parent or guardian to do this.

(✓) We'll send your certificate via
email and you'll receive a brilliant
badge through the post!